# CRABTREE CONTACT

# THE HISTORY OF HIP HOP

Melanie J. Cornish

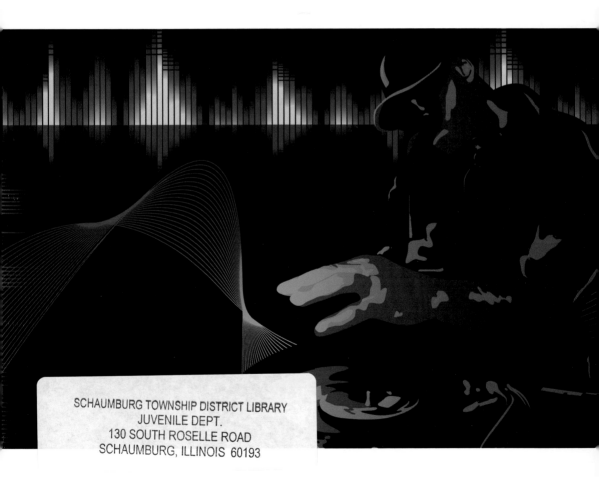

 Crabtree Publishing Company

www.crabtreebooks.com

## Crabtree Publishing Company

www.crabtreebooks.com          1-800-387-7650
Copyright © **2009 CRABTREE PUBLISHING COMPANY.**

**Published
in Canada
Crabtree Publishing**
616 Welland Ave.
St. Catharines, ON
L2M 5V6

**Published in the
United States
Crabtree Publishing**
PMB16A
350 Fifth Ave., Suite 3308
New York, NY  10118

Content development by Shakespeare Squared
www.ShakespeareSquared.com

**Author**: Melanie J. Cornish
**Project editor**: Ruth Owen
**Project designer**: Simon Fenn
**Photo research**: Ruth Owen
**Project coordinator**: Robert Walker
**Production coordinator**: Katherine Berti
**Prepress technicians**: Samara Parent,
   Katherine Berti, Ken Wright

Thank you to
Lorraine Petersen
and the members
of nasen

**Picture credits**:
Corbis: Jerry Arcieri: p. 12
David Corio: p. 6 (bottom), 18
diverseimages.net: Chi Modu: p. 21, 22
Getty Images: p. 7, 8, 19 (bottom), 24, 25, 26–27, 29;
   Michael Ochs Archive: p. 9, 16–17, 19 (top), 20, 23
Clayton Hauck: p. 28
Ernest Paniccioli: p. 6 (top)
Monifa Perry: p. 11
Shutterstock: front cover, p. 1, 2–3, 4–5, 12 (background),
   13, 14–15, 18-19 (background), 31

Every effort has been made to trace copyright holders, and we apologize in
advance for any omissions. We would be pleased to insert the appropriate
acknowledgments in any subsequent edition of this publication.

**Library and Archives Canada Cataloguing in Publication**

Cornish, Melanie J.
    History of hip hop / Melanie J. Cornish.

(Crabtree contact)
Includes index.
ISBN 978-0-7787-3820-6 (bound).--ISBN 978-0-7787-3841-1 (pbk.)

    1. Rap (Music)--History and criticism--Juvenile literature.
2. Hip-hop--Juvenile literature. I. Title. II. Series: Crabtree contact

ML3531.C818 2009      j782.42164909      C2008-907848-9

**Library of Congress Cataloging-in-Publication Data**

Cornish, Melanie J.
   History of hip hop / Melanie J. Cornish.
      p. cm. -- (Crabtree contact)
   Includes index.
   ISBN 978-0-7787-3841-1 (pbk. : alk. paper) -- ISBN
978-0-7787-3820-6 (reinforced library binding : alk. paper)
   1. Rap (Music)--History and criticism--Juvenile literature.
   2. Hip-hop--Juvenile literature. I. Title. II. Series.

   ML3531.C666 2009
   782.42164909--dc22

                                          2008052406

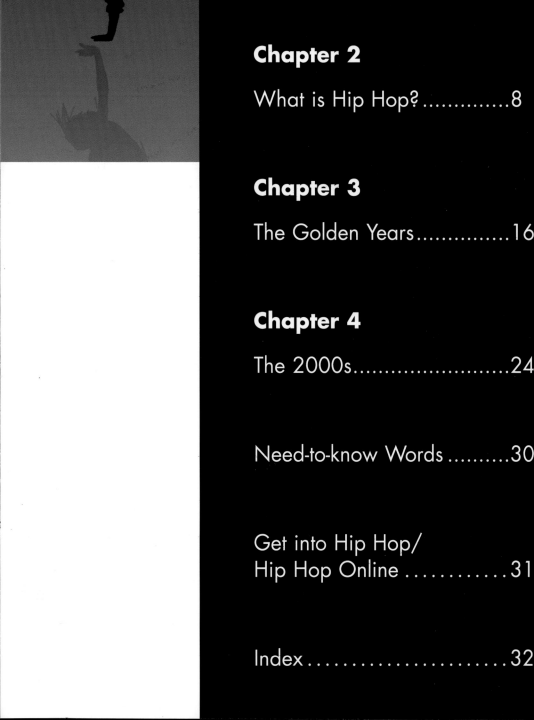

# CHAPTER 1

# WHERE IT ALL BEGAN

Hip hop began in the early 1970s. It began on the streets of the South Bronx, in New York City.

Since then, hip hop **culture** has brought people together from all over the world. They celebrate and enjoy hip hop music and break dancing.

Today, people perform hip hop all over the world. In many places, it has moved from the street corner to the stage.

A man named DJ Kool Herc helped hip hop get its start.

Kool Herc is a **DJ** in New York. DJs play records or CDs for an audience to listen to or dance to. In the early 1970s, Kool Herc started to hold **block parties** in his neighborhood.

DJ Kool Herc

Hundreds of adults and children went to Herc's block parties. He played music at the parties. So did another DJ named Grandmaster Flash.

In 1973, DJ Kool Herc's sister, Cindy Campbell, had a house party. The party was at 1520 Sedgwick Avenue.

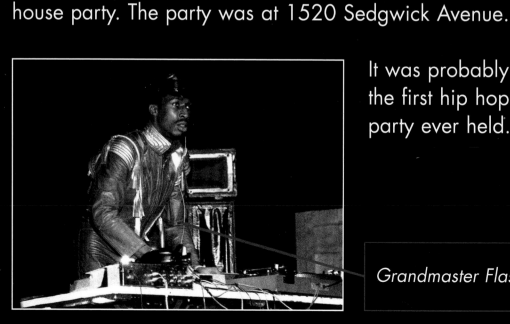

It was probably the first hip hop party ever held.

Grandmaster Flash

The party put 1520 Sedgwick Avenue on the map as the birthplace of hip hop.

1520 SEDGWICK AVE.

# CHAPTER 2

# WHAT IS HIP HOP?

There are four important parts to hip hop.

## THE MC

An **MC** is an artist who writes rhymes or poems. Then, he or she raps (says) them over a beat.

**Emceeing** began in Africa. African poets delivered their folk tales over drums and other instruments.

*Rakim was the first MC to use internal rhyming. This means he uses more patterns than normal within the bars of a song.*

In 1979, the Sugarhill Gang released the single Rapper's Delight. It was the first **"Gold"** selling record in hip hop. It sold over 500,000 copies.

*Rapper's Delight* was even heard in countries that had no idea what hip hop was!

The song was a big hit around the world and...

...people wanted to hear more.

| Wonder Mike | Master Gee | Big Bank Hank |

 Sugarhill Gang made dreams come true for those of us who couldn't sing or dance.

MC Ice Cube

The DJ gives the MC a musical background against which to perform his or her poetry.

Hip hop DJs learned to make different sounds using the needles on their turntables.

DJs such as Grandmaster Flash, Caz, and Grand Wizard Theodore invented scratching.

Scratching is when a DJ plays a very short part of a song backward and forward. A DJ does this by moving the record using his or her hand.

New York based DJ Scratch is famous for his scratching **techniques**.

 I still get excited when I hear my music on the radio today, and it's been over 20 years since I started.

*DJ Scratch*

DJ Scratch

As hip hop music spread through the streets, parks, and schools of the U.S., a new style of dancing developed. It was called "break dancing."

Break dancing combines fast footwork, gymnastics, and freezes. Freezes are when the dancer stops moving and holds a **stylish** or difficult pose for a few seconds.

The dancers became known as B-Boys and B-Girls. They developed their dances alongside the hip hop MCs and DJs.

Break dancers were often part of groups called "crews."

Crews would have dancing "battles." The crowd would decide who was the best crew.

A B-Girl freezes

# THE GRAFFITI ARTIST

**Graffiti** art is also a part of hip hop culture.

Graffiti artists use spray paint to paint large, colorful words and images.

New York City became a center for graffiti art at the same time as hip hop became popular. Graffiti became linked with hip hop.

Graffiti artists created art in places where DJs and MCs were making music.

Like emceeing and break dancing, graffiti
is a way for people to express themselves.

Sometimes a graffiti artist is asked to
create a large piece of artwork called
a mural. A mural can brighten up a
building or neighborhood.

A graffiti artist must always have
permission before he or she paints
on a building.

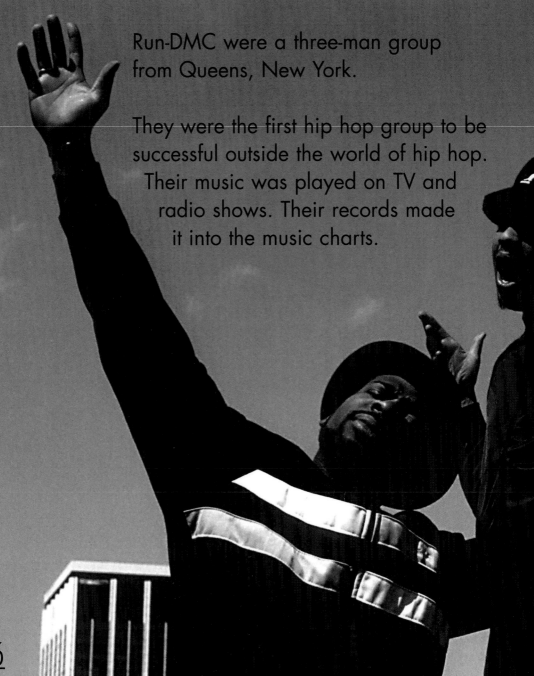

# CHAPTER 3

# THE GOLDEN YEARS

For many hip hop fans the mid-1980s to mid-1990s are a special time in hip hop's history. Many important hip hop artists began making records during this time.

Run-DMC were a three-man group from Queens, New York.

They were the first hip hop group to be successful outside the world of hip hop. Their music was played on TV and radio shows. Their records made it into the music charts.

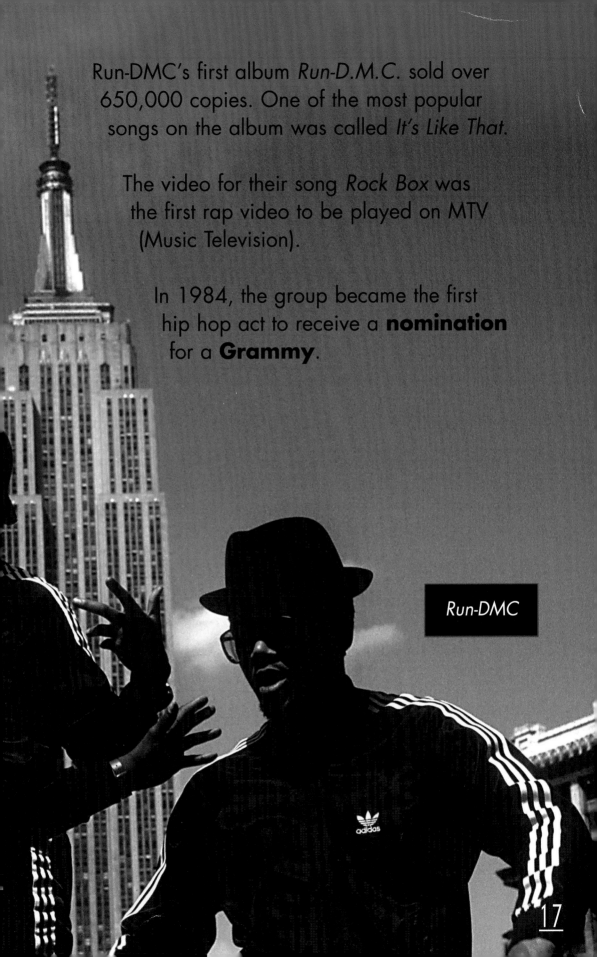

Run-DMC's first album *Run-D.M.C.* sold over 650,000 copies. One of the most popular songs on the album was called *It's Like That*.

The video for their song *Rock Box* was the first rap video to be played on MTV (Music Television).

In 1984, the group became the first hip hop act to receive a **nomination** for a **Grammy**.

Run-DMC

Big Daddy Kane
was a rapper from
Brooklyn, New York.

His songs talked about
Africa and the history of
African-Americans.

His songs also talked
about how good
his own song
**lyrics** were!

Big Daddy
Kane was the
first person
to start hip hop
fashion trends.
He wore sweat
suits and large
gold rings.
Other hip hop
artists copied
his style.

*Big Daddy Kane*

Nine of LL Cool J's albums have gone "**Platinum**." This means an album has sold over one million copies in the U.S.

LL Cool J is also a successful actor. He has starred in movies such as the football movie, *Any Given Sunday*.

LL Cool J

Will Smith and DJ Jazzy Jeff

DJ Jazzy Jeff and rapper The Fresh Prince (Will Smith) met in their hometown of Philadelphia.

Their second album, *He's the DJ, I'm the Rapper*, won them a Grammy award.

Today, Will Smith is one of the world's most famous movie actors. DJ Jazzy Jeff works with other hip hop artists helping them make records.

In the late 1980s and early 1990s, some new hip hop groups began to focus on gang life and violence. This style of hip hop became known as "**gangsta rap**."

Groups, such as N.W.A, talked about the issues some young people face living in inner cities.

Their lyrics talked about kids joining gangs and conflict between young people and the police.

However, other top hip hop groups used their music to spread positive and inspiring messages.

*Arrested Development*

Arrested Development was a group of artists from Atlanta, Georgia.

Their positive lyrics talked about equal rights and the Earth. Their lyrics were the opposite of the gangsta rap lyrics.

A Tribe Called Quest was another group from Queens, New York. The group was made up of two rappers and their DJ.

The group's song lyrics were lighthearted and positive. Their songs talked about life as a carefree teenager.

The group's message to their fans was "just be yourself."

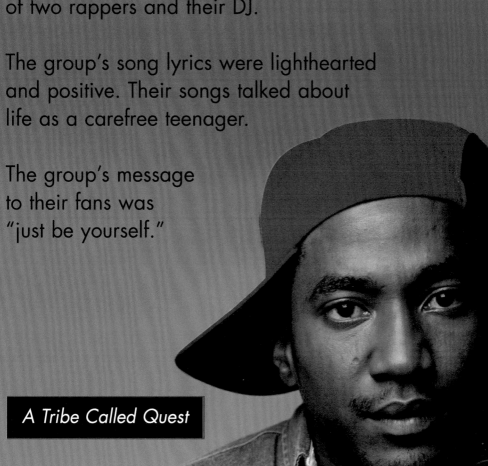

*A Tribe Called Quest*

Throughout hip hop's history, most of its stars have been men. However, some female artists have been very successful.

Queen Latifah is often called "The Queen of Rap."

She began releasing records in the late 1980s and became a big hip hop star.

Queen Latifah

Queen Latifah is also a successful actress. She has starred in movies and TV shows.

Salt-N-Pepa and DJ Spinderella were the most successful female hip hop act in history.

They had male and female fans all over the world.

Salt-N-Pepa released five albums and sold over 13 million records. They also won five Grammy awards.

*Salt-N-Pepa and DJ Spinderella in 1988*

# CHAPTER 4

# THE 2000s

In the 2000s, hip hop music is more successful than ever. Today, many rap artists, such as Jay Z and Nelly, are not just known for their music. These hip hop artists are also big celebrities!

*Nelly*

Nelly is a very successful rapper from St. Louis, Missouri. He has made four albums and sold over 50 million copies of his records.

Nelly could have played professional baseball.

*Jay Z and Beyoncé perform together in 2003*

In 2008, Jay Z performed at the famous music festival at Glastonbury, in the UK. He was the first hip hop artist to be the main act at the festival.

He was watched by 100,000 fans and his superstar wife, Beyoncé.

Missy Elliot is a popular rapper. She has been making records since the early 1990s.

Missy Elliot has had six Platinum albums. She has also won five Grammy awards for her music.

Missy Elliott has also been successful as a songwriter and producer for other artists.

As a **producer**, Missy Elliott helps other artists create and record their songs.

She has worked with artists such as Mariah Carey, Janet Jackson, Aaliyah, and Mary J. Blige.

*Missy Elliott wins an award at the 2007 VH1 Hip Hop Honors ceremony*

Today, some rappers put their music on the Internet. Fans can listen to the music online. Fans can buy the music online, too.

The Internet allows new groups to sell their music without the help of a record **label**.

The Cool Kids are a hip hop group from Chicago and Detroit. They put their music on their *MySpace.com* page.

Their online success got them a recording deal with a record label.

Antoine (Mikey Rocks) Reed (top) and Evan (Chuck Inglish) Ingersoll

Today, some MCs are more than just musical superstars. They have also become very successful business people.

Sean "Diddy" Combs has businesses in the music industry. He also owns restaurants, and has produced lines of clothing, shoes, and even wheels for cars!

# NEED-TO-KNOW WORDS

**block party** An informal, outdoor party where people from a neighborhood come together and dance while a DJ plays music

**culture** A way of life or a set of beliefs or shared interests and values that bring a group of people together

**DJ** A person who plays records or CDs for an audience or a person who hosts a radio show. DJ is short for Disc Jockey

**emceeing** Rapping (saying) words over a musical background

**gangsta rap** A type of hip hop music that talked about the issues kids faced in inner cities

**Gold** When a record has sales of over 500,000 in the U.S. and over 100,000 in the UK

**graffiti** Colorful words and artwork created using spray paint

**Grammy** An award given to music acts by the "National Academy of Recording Arts and Sciences." It is awarded to artists for their records or because their work is considered important in the music world

**label** A record company

**lyrics** The words of a song

**MC** This is short for "Master of Ceremonies." MCs are people who host a show and introduce acts. In the hip hop world, an MC is another name for a rapper

**nomination** To be one of the people put forward for an award

**Platinum** When a record has sales of over one million in the U.S. and over 300,000 in the UK.

**producer** A person who works with music artists in a recording studio to help them create their music

**stylish** Describing something that is popular among those who set trends

**technique** A way of accomplishing something

# GET INTO HIP HOP

If you are interested in getting into the hip hop business, here are some tips.

- Use websites such as *MySpace.com* to get your music noticed. Labels sometimes use these websites to find new artists.

- If you write your own lyrics, make sure you copyright your material. Copyrighting means you officially own the lyrics and no one else can use them without your permission. See www.copyright.gov

- Apply for summer jobs at record labels and magazines. You might have to work for free, but these jobs can help you make good contacts. Check the law where you live to make sure you are old enough to have a job.

# HIP HOP ONLINE

www.DaveyD.com
The website of hip hop journalist Davey D

www.rocksteadycrew.com
The website of the world's most famous B-Boy crew

# INDEX

Printed in the U.S.A. - BG